I Am Still Standing

A guide to God, love,
healing,
deliverance
And blessings!

✝✝✝

by Yolanda N. Harris

ISBN: 978-1-938950-64-3

Editor: Shari Armstrong
Interior Design: Tony Bradford

Greater is He Publishing
9824 E. Washington St,
Chagrin Falls Ohio 44023
P O. Box 46115
Bedford Ohio, 44146

Acknowledgments:

I want to give all honor and praise to God. For without God I would not have been able to document these words that He placed in my spirit. God has taken me on such a tremendous journey to bring me where I am today. It has not been an easy journey, but it is a well worth it journey.

I want to recognize my leaders, who without them I would not be where I am. Apostle Arnell Smith and the late Mother JimElla Smith laid the foundation for my spiritual walk. They guided me down the path of righteousness and taught me to listen to the voice of God. They had always encouraged me to live my dreams and allow God to use me. Apostle Arnell Smith continues to be a vital instrument in my walk with God.

God as now placed Pastor Robert Madison and First Lady Traci Madison as my leaders to guide me in the next level of my life. You both have always encouraged me, stood by me, prayed for me, and kept me lifted up to the Father in the gift and ministry He has birthed in me. I will always remain grateful for your sacrifice, love, and time that you have shown me.

Dedication:

I dedicate this book to my beautiful daughter Keranie. You have been such a breath of fresh air in my life. I didn't think I could have children but God showed me a miracle when He blessed me with you. I strive to do better and be better for you. I know we have our moments but they don't outweigh the blessings God has bestowed upon us. I am proud to be your mother and want nothing but the best for you. I love you with all my heart and soul. Stay encouraged. Keep your eyes lifted always to God and He will guide you.

Love Always,

Mommy

Contents

I've been down too long
Up against the wall
Fighting for my life.

I've been down too long
Taking the devil's blows
Trying to take my life
He's backed me up
I can't move no more
Trying to take me out
Nothing seems real clear
I'm full of fear
Fighting for my life, my life.

I'm up against the wall
With nowhere to turn
Trying to find a way out

I feel so alone
Like all hope is gone
Trying to stay alive
My mind is gone

Trying to keep holding on
By God's grace I'm here, I'm here.

God is fighting for my life
My purpose must be great
My soul belongs to thee
My Lord, the Lord
The one and only God
Come and set me free
From the burdens of this world
Cause your fighting for my life, my life.

You've been down too long
Up against the wall
Fighting for your life, your life.

✝

My Life Commentary

We as carnal minded individuals are always trying to do everything on our own. But Christ came and died on the cross for all our sins, healings, deliverances, heartaches and pains. "The thief cometh not, but to steal, and to kill, and to destroy: I am come that they might have life, and that they might have it more abundantly." (John 10:10 KJV) Yes we shall endure test and trials, but they don't come to destroy us but to build us up, make us stronger, and to bring us closer to God. We are living a spiritual warfare temporarily living in a fleshly body. Earth is not our home, heaven is. God said, "And he said, Hearken ye, all Judah, and ye inhabitants of Jerusalem, and thou king Jehoshaphat, Thus saith the Lord unto you, Be not afraid nor dismayed by reason of this great multitude; for the battle is not yours, but God's." (2 Chronicles 20:15 KJV) We can't fight everything, but those things we can God has equipped us with the full armor. The word's tells us to put on the full armor of God. (Ephesians 6:11-17) "Put on the whole armour of God, that ye may be able to stand against the wiles of the devil. For we wrestle not against flesh and blood, but against principalities, against powers, against the rulers of the darkness of this world, against spiritual wickedness in high places. Wherefore take unto you the whole armour of God, that ye may be able to withstand in the evil day, and having done all, to stand. Stand therefore, having your loins girt about with truth, and having on the breastplate of righteousness; And your feet shod with the preparation of the gospel of peace; Above all, taking the shield of faith, wherewith ye shall be able to quench all the fiery darts of the wicked. And take the helmet of salvation, and the sword of the Spirit, which is the word of God:"

God loves us so much that He created and prepared this earth with everything we could ever need or want. We as sinners have caused our environment to be as it is. God revealed to me that we always have heard that we are a product of our environment, but how is that possible when the environment was created perfect. The environment is a product of us. We have caused the environment to be what it is from our sin. God gave us dominion over the land and we have not done such a great job have we? The enemy is in his dwelling place here on earth and he is "seeking whom he may devour" (I Peter 5:8 KJV). Pick up your armor brother and sister and be ready to fight the good fight of faith.

The enemy will press us up against the wall, but we can press our way out. God has our back and He will not let us fall. We let us fall. We get in the way of what God is trying to do. We try to live according to our will and not God's. Remember that, "For my thoughts are not your thoughts, neither are your ways my ways, saith the Lord." (Isaiah 55:8 KJV) When God created us we were perfect, sin is what separate us from Him. We will continue to sin while we are in this fleshly body, but we are to repent and turn from our wicked ways. Each day we are to become more like Christ. There are many temptations in this world that will constantly try to trip us up, but we must stand and continue to stay focused on the prize and that

4

is heaven and everlasting life with God. Be encouraged today my brother and sister and know that God loves us and only wants the best for us. This too shall pass.

Over the years I have always heard and even said; "this is my life and I'll do what I want to do"! When we are living in the world our lives belong to Satan. When we are living for God our lives belong to Him. If you haven't noticed, there is no middle man. There is no luke warm, either you are hot or cold. There is no straddling the fence either you are living for God or you're not. God said: "And if it seem evil unto you to serve the Lord, choose you this day whom ye will serve; whether the gods which your fathers served that were on the other side of the flood, or the gods of the Amorites, in whose land ye dwell: but as for me and my house, we will serve the Lord." (Joshua 24:15 KJV) God don't want half of you, he wants all of you. Have you heard of the song: "99 ½ won't do"? Keep running towards 100 because that is what He is looking for. "For thou shalt worship no other god: for the Lord, whose name is jealous, is a jealous God." (Exodus 34:14 KJV) Our life was bought with a price when Christ went to the cross. You are not your own anymore. When we decide in our heart's to get saved, and live for God we are no longer ours but the Lords. There is a life change that must come when we live for God. Though we live in the world, we are not to be a part of the world and do as the world does. We are to become a separated people and stand out amongst the lost. We are the light to those that are trapped in darkness. God is soon to return for His church that has no spot or wrinkle. Are you still swaying back and forth allowing your flesh to make all the decisions for you? Your flesh shall return to the dust from wince it was created and your soul shall return to the dwelling place of judgment to determine where you shall

5

spend eternity. According to your walk, where does your eternity lye?

We spend so much time worrying about what other people think or what they are doing. We spend so much time trying to fit in instead of standing out. We are to become more like Christ daily has our minds are renewed by the washing of the word and the spirit of God. If we are still cursing, smoking, drinking, hanging out in the clubs/bars, cheating, fornicating, lying, gossiping, backbiting, etc., we have not truly turned our hearts and lives over to God. Because when you truly get saved and baptized in the Holy Ghost there will be change in your life style (a character change). It is time to have a character change. Your character will begin to change when you begin to apply the fruits of the Spirit. (Galatians 5:22-23) Others will be able to recognize which fruits you are working in. The more the fruits abide in you the more you abide in the Lord. If you are not carrying the fruits of the Spirit then you remain in the darkness. Only the enemy dwells in the dark places, God is in the light.

We are in search of love, happiness, joy, and a peace of mind. Only God provides those things. The enemy brings false love, happiness, joy and peace of mind then he breaks you down to destroy you. Don't be deceived by his cunning ways. Come out from amongst them that reside in the darkness and be reborn again into the light. Begin to study the word of God and allow Him to give you revelation of who you are and who He is. You will begin to find yourself and realize your place in the Kingdom. The enemy has kept you in the dark long enough, it's time to fight for your life and rise up against the prince of darkness. It's time to stop living haphazardly and as a child. Christ was crucified, died, and rose again so you may live. Are you ready to live?

Prayer

Father God I pray for my brother and sister today. I bind strongholds of the mind. They are the head and not the tail. They can do all things through Christ who strengthens you. There is no weapon that will form against them that shall prosper. God I pray that their mind is renewed daily by diving in your word, getting the understanding of your word, worshipping your holy name, praying without ceasing until their breakthrough comes forth, and that they don't forget to assemble themselves with other believers. Father I thank you for their freedom and deliverance of everything that is not like you. May they become new creatures in Christ Jesus.

Amen

My Testimony

I didn't grow up in the church. I didn't know who God was. I saw many people go to church but came home doing the same ole stuff, living the same ole way. There was no change or difference in their life style or character. I went through sexual abuse, mental abuse, and verbal abuse. I grew up looking for love in everything. I began drinking when I was twelve hoping it would cause everything around me to stop. I began giving myself sexually when I was fifteen. I felt so empty and alone. I started smoking marijuana and cigarettes when I was fifteen too. I also ate all the time to hide from my true feelings, but nothing seemed to work. I was miserable and I was crying out for help. Then I was introduced to the one and only true living God when I was eighteen. Throughout the years I was still trying to live my life the way I wanted, my flesh was fighting, but after a while I finally realized this

7

ɔnger my life. Once I had given my heart and soul couldn't run from him. You see Jesus is married to the ɔ slider. I thank God that he never left me. Since then I have matured and grown stronger in my faith and I am now living my life fully for the Lord. It is no longer my life but His. I thank you God for salvation, restoration, forgiveness, and for Your grace and mercy. I thank God for having a desire to want to be closer to Him and to live for Him. I don't desire the things of the world anymore. This walk has truly been a journey.

Share your testimony.

_____

_____

_____

_____

_____

_____

_____

_____

_____

_____

CHAPTER 2
Send Your Blessings

Send your blessings down Lord
And I'll praise your name
Send your blessings down Lord
And I'll praise your name

I'll praise you in the AM
I'll praise you in the noonday
I'll praise you in the PM
And I'll praise your name

I'll praise you in the good
I'll praise you in the bad
I'll even praise you when I'm sad
And I'll praise your name

I'll praise you because you're holy
I'll praise you because you're worthy
I'll praise you because you love me
And I'll praise your name

I'll praise you everywhere I go
I'll praise you even in my sleep
I'll praise you when I'm alone
And I'll praise your name

Send your blessings down Lord
And I'll praise your name
Send your blessings down Lord
And I'll praise your name

✝

Send Your Blessings Commentary

There are many blessings that we can receive on a daily basis. One blessing is that God allows us to wake up every day, because there are individuals who did not wake up. God wants to shower us with blessings daily, but if He feels that we aren't ready we aren't going to get them until we are. Remember it's in His timing not ours. God ask, "Why would I give you a $1,000 when you can't handle a $100". There are individuals that continue to beg God for things even though God has already told them no. After a while He will allow the blessing to birth prematurely to please them, and because the blessing is premature the individual as no idea how to handle it. They didn't allow themselves to finish preparation to receive the blessing. Therefore the blessing will fall to the waist side and not handled in the position God designed for them too. We need to learn to appreciate what we have instead of wishing and asking for more. God always gives us exactly what we need, but it's the wants that keep us searching for more. Then we keep our eyes focused on others and their blessings and becoming jealous and desiring what they have. We must learn to be happy when others are being blessed, because that will show compassion, love, and a heart for others and their happiness. Everything is not about us.

Also God wants us to keep our spiritual eyes open when it comes to blessings because the enemy sends false blessings as well. This is where the spirit of discernment should be flowing. Don't focus on the blessings because that will keep us hindered and add more sorrow than good. Our ambition should be to, "I press toward the mark for the prize of the high calling of God in Christ Jesus." (Philippians 3:14 KJV) Let us begin to pray, have faith and believe that God is taking care of us. God will deliver, heal, forgive, and bless us when we ask. A closed mouth doesn't get fed. But God is not going to bless mess. We need to ask God to prepare us to be ready to receive our blessings because they will be more than we have room for. When asking God to bless us we must ask with a pure heart, with good intentions, and the right motives. "And it shall come to pass, if thou shalt hearken diligently unto the voice of the Lord thy God, to observe and to do all his commandments which I command thee this day, that the Lord thy God will set thee on high above all nations of the earth: And all these blessings shall come on thee, and overtake thee, if thou shalt hearken unto the voice of the Lord thy God. Blessed shalt thou be in the city, and blessed shalt thou be in the field." (Deuteronomy 28 KJV) God's promise to bless us will come forth rather it is here on this earth or in heaven. Do not be dismayed or wearer, God knows what we need and what we desire, "Before I formed thee in the belly I knew thee; and before thou camest forth out of the womb I sanctified thee, and I ordained thee a prophet unto the nations." (Jeremiah 1:5 KJV) God knows everything about us because He is omnipresent (present everywhere at the same time) and omniscient (everything). He is the creator of ALL.

God's desire is to bless us and for us to be happy. We question on why we don't have certain things like others or why we are going through circumstances and others don't seem to be going through anything. The grass is not always greener on the other side. A lot of times we don't know what trials they have suffered and the sacrifices they have made to gain the blessings they have. Many can put on a fake façade and have others believing that they have it all together. So we must not base our walk with Christ by watching others. Salvation is an individual walk and relationship with Lord that we have to work for. Blessings come according to the call on one's life, their works, their fruits, and their walk with Christ. We are not perfect, we will slip and fall, and we will make mistakes. But what we do after all that is what truly matters. Pick yourself up and keep going, don't give up on God, because He won't give up on you.

Every day we need to rise and thank God for blessing us to see yet another day. He allowed us to have use of our limbs. We are in our right mind. We have a roof over our heads. We have food on our table. We have clothes on our backs. Our utilities are on. We have transportation. Do you see the many blessings we already have? But we become greedy and start wishing and begging for more stuff. Are we ever satisfied? Did you know that when we become content with what you have and where you are that is when God really starts to shower you with His blessings? The reason is we have taken the focus off the blessing and have turned our focus towards Him. God said make your request known and He will take it from there. He knows our wants and desires and will supply them as long as they line up with the plan and will He has for our lives. It's not like God doesn't want us to have nice things or go nice places. He just doesn't want those things to be the driving force in our lives or for them to overtake us. Like my Pastor always says (Pastor Robert Madison) "God blesses you

15

with that BMW and now you decide to take a drive to show it off. Well the day you decide to take that ride just so happen to be on Sunday during your service time. Don't allow the blessing to keep you from God, the one who blessed you with it." He wants to be what drives us. Also we need to praise Him even without the blessings. We need to bless Him daily for just who He is, because without Him we are nothing. We wouldn't even exist if it wasn't for Him. So let us begin to praise Him in *ALL* things.

Prayer

Father God I pray that your people pray selflessly for your blessings. I pray that they begin to seek the kingdom above all things and will to do your work. Continue to send your Angels of Protection and cover them with the blood. God I pray that they begin to have a mind and heart like Christ and only want the things of God. Send your blessings according to your will and your way. I thank you Lord and worship your name.

Amen

Testimony

For years I didn't think I could have children. I was married when I was 24 years old. We had become pregnant, but going on our third month I had a miscarriage. The doctor said it was a deteriorated egg. I went through that miscarriage for a week. My heart was broken and my spirits crushed. I wanted to be a mom so bad. Of course I questioned why me? God why won't you allow me to have a baby? Why do you keep allowing others to have children that don't want them or they hurt them? So after 9 years I told God that if it's not in his plan for me to be a mom I am content with my life now. I was backslidden at the time and living a haphazard life. But even in that God blessed me with my Miracle and I became pregnant. Of course the first three months the enemy kept me in fear with the bleeding. But God used my baby to remind me that she is my miracle and was here to stay. During an ultrasound she waved at me to say I'm here mom. My beautiful little girl is now 3 years old. She is my miracle. I am grateful and blessed to be a mom and even more because

I never thought I could be one. I am honored He gave me the privilege to become a mom. I thank you Lord for your blessings.

Share your testimony

_____

_____

_____

_____

_____

_____

_____

_____

_____

20

CHAPTER 3

Get Up and Praise the Lord

Get up and praise the Lord
Get up and praise the Lord
Get up and praise the Lord
Today, Today

Don't wait until tomorrow
Tomorrow's not promised to you
Don't wait until tonight
Tonight's not promised to you
Don't wait for the next hour
The hour's not promised to you
You alt to get up and praise the Lord

Don't wait for your family
Don't wait for your friends
Don't wait until it's good
Or until the end
Don't wait until the trials are over
Or until your well
You alt to get up and praise the Lord

If the Lord has brought you out
From what had you bound

If the Lord has set you free
From the enemy
If the Lord gave his Son
Just to show you love
You alt to get up and praise the Lord

Get up and Praise the Lord
Get up and Praise the Lord
Get up and Praise the Lord
Today, Today

✝

Get Up and Praise the Lord Commentary

Each day that we rise God deserves to be praised. "This is the day which the Lord hath made; we will rejoice and be glad in it." (Psalm 118:24 KJV) We are not promised to see tomorrow. Our days are numbered and only God knows when that number is up. There are many who haven't even heard the name of Jesus. It is the saint's job to preach the gospel of Jesus Christ and salvation to all. There are many who have grown up in the church but still live their lives according to the world and not the word. Individuals decide to stay where they are worshipping because they have been there since they were young and they are comfortable there. If you are comfortable where you worship then the Holy Ghost isn't moving there. We should not be comfortable in our sin and sitting in the presence of God.

God loves us so much that, "For God so loved the world, that he gave his only begotten Son, that whosoever believeth in him should not perish, but have everlasting life." (John 3:16 KJV) We question on why so many are dying. Well we are now living in the end times, and we must remember that this earth is the home of the enemy and he is, "seeking who he may devour" (I Peter 5:8 KJV). Also we must remember that as long as we live in a sinful world bad things will continue to happen. God is calling His people to come forth and prepare to go home to heaven. We must praise God in the good and in the bad. We must praise God rather we feel like it or not. God honors our praise when it comes from our hearts. "Praise ye the Lord. Praise God in his sanctuary: praise him in the firmament of his power. Praise him for his mighty acts: praise him according to his excellent greatness. Praise him with the sound of the trumpet: praise him with the psaltery and harp." (Psalm 150 KJV)

God wants us to be happy and blessed while we reside here on this earth. But we must be mindful that this earth will soon pass away and a new heaven and new earth will then exist. We must live each day according to God's word and commandments. We must live each day worshipping and praising God. "Jesus saith unto him, I am the way, the truth, and the life: no man cometh unto the Father, but by me." (John 14:6 KJV) Come to God before it is too late. God is calling you today.

Many congregations go to church every Sunday for a show. They anticipate the praise and worship part of the service so they can sing, clap their hands and show off their moves. So what is the true motive behind their praise? Are they truly praising and worshipping God or are they just keeping up with the Jones's? God don't want a show or a fake praise, he wants your pure heart. Then there are congregations where you have those dignified folk that feel like that's just too much. Dignified folks feel as though" it don't take all that" to praise and worship God. Then there are individuals who just go to church because this is what they have done since they were little, so it has become religion. Then you have the spectators who sit back and just watch everyone else worshipping and praising God while they remain full of their mess.

So is your praise real and pure? Do you just wait until Sunday to praise and worship God? Is Sunday the only day you open your bible, or do you even bring them then? Many have gotten out of the habits of bringing their bibles to church, and they rely solely on what is being preached. Many are too busy texting, Facebooking, Tweeting, or video recording the service to even concentrate or pay attention to the Word that is being preached. Are you only attending church to socialize, show off your new outfit, or out of religion? God desires for us to talk to Him daily, to get in His word daily, and to praise and worship Him daily. Let's turn the radio off and allow the spirit of God to have His way. Let's cancel the concert and give this time to lift God up. Sometimes we must be still and be quiet so we can hear from God. We miss out on what God is saying to us because we are too loud and so is the environment we are in. Are you ready to listen to God?

Prayer

Father God, I pray for your people today. I pray that they have the desire to want to live saved and live their life fully for you. I pray that they will see the deception that the enemy as blinded them with. Father I pray that they begin to desire you Lord and your way. I pray that they no longer desire the things of the world. I bind the enemy from all evil deeds that he is trying to strike on each individual. I command him to flee from the minds, hearts, and souls of your people. I pray for complete deliverance, healing, and freedom from the wiles of the devil. God I thank you for what you are doing for your people. I thank You for answering prayer, in Jesus mighty name.

Amen

Testimony

There are many times that my flesh doesn't feel like doing anything. But I have noticed when I push through my feelings and sacrifice, than I feel better in my spirit. When I go to service I can feel the spirit all over me and just can't sit there. I don't see how others just sit in their seats and not get up to praise the Lord. I may praise him in dance, song, clapping my hands, or just worshipping him. I also praise God in my writing. There are several ways we can get up and worship God. When I rise in the morning, when I am bathing, when I am washing dishes, when I'm driving, even when I am working I give praise to God. God is just looking for a selfless, joy filled, heart felt praise. Don't get so busy you forget to talk to God. God wants to fellowship with us so we may know who He is. I am so amazed every time God reveals His secrets to me. I feel honored that He trusts me with that important information. I have begun to praise and worship God daily. I hunger God now.

Share your testimony

_____

_____

_____

_____

_____

_____

_____

_____

_____

_____

Hello Lord
How are you today
I give you the praise
And I worship your name
I honor you Lord
For you are worthy of all the praise

You are God
You are God
And I worship your name

Wonderful and true
The best at what you do
Merciful and kind
Never leaving me behind
Patient and loving
Majestic and mine

You are God
You are God
And I honor your name

With just the mention of your name

It brightens up my day
The tenderness of your voice
Puts a smile on my face
And I know
Everything will be okay
To get in your presence and
Worship you, just because of who you are

You are God
You are God
And I worship your name

You are God
You are God
And I honor your name

✝

Hello Lord Commentary

Each day we need to speak to God and talk to Him just like we talk to one of our friends. God wants to have an individual relationship with us. We are unique and one of a kind and God deals with us differently. God appreciates when we think about Him instead of ourselves all the time. Come with a humble heart and spirit and remember that God took time to create you. "And God said," Let us make man in our image, after our likeness: and let them have dominion over the fish of the sea, and over the fowl of the air, and over the cattle, and over all the earth, and over every creeping thing that creepeth upon the earth." (Genesis 1:26 KJV) God was pleased with His creation and He saw it was good. God was so excited to create us. He placed us in a special garden and gave us everything that we could ever need or want. God still desires to do so. But sin came in and separated us from Him. God has not turned His back on us, but He desires for us to want Him without force. He longs for our love. God loves us so much even after our sin that He sent His son, Jesus. "For God so loved the world, that he gave his only begotten Son, that whosoever believeth in him should not perish, but have everlasting life." (John 10:10 KJV) God gave us an outlet to be able to have another chance of eternal life with Him and that is through His Son Jesus Christ.

God wants nothing more but to have His creation desire and want a relationship with Him. He already knows that each creation will not enter into the gates of heaven, but He will be pleased with those that chose to follow and love Him. Love God today and show Him. We can show Him by staying in our word, talking to Him daily, and living our lives according to His word. We can show Him by denying ourselves and lifting Him up. We can also show Him by the way we treat other people. "Then said Jesus unto his disciples, if any man will come after me, let him deny himself, and take up his cross, and follow me." (Matthew 16:24 KJV) We must worship and praise God in the good and in the bad, but let us worship Him just because of who He is. God is the almighty, one and only true living God. There are no other god's before Him.

Have you ever just sat back and thought about the creator? How detailed and perfect God is? How awesome He is? No one can ever duplicate what He has done no matter how much they try. Let us just worship God for who He is. We would not exist if it wasn't for Him. He had the desire to create us and make this world. Each sin, each negative thought, each denial, each lifeless prayers keeps us separated from Him. "And if it seems evil unto you to serve the Lord, choose you this day whom ye will serve; whether the gods which your fathers served that were on the other side of the flood, or the gods of the Amorites, in whose land ye dwell: but as for me and my house, we will serve the Lord." (Joshua 24:15 KJV)

When you rise in the morning what is your first thought, first spoken word, or first written word? Do you thank God for allowing you to see yet another day? Do you thank God for allowing you to see, to have the use of your limbs, or for even being in your right mind? We have so many

things that we can rise up and thank God for. How much time out of our day do we even think about the blessings that surrounds us? Being grateful is more than just about material things. What exactly are you grateful for? Do you truly know what blessings are? Do you even feel blessed by God or do you feel that you do everything on your own and that's why you're blessed?

There are so many questions that we must ask ourselves. But are we ready to answer them? Are we ready to get closer to God? Are we ready to do what it takes to have a relationship with God? Let us get started right now. Put the book down and begin to talk to God right now. He is ready to hear everything that you have to say. He is ready to hear your cries, your hopes, your dreams, your needs, your wants, your desires and anything else that may be on your mind or in your heart. Don't be shy, be free. Get in the presence of God and pour your heart out to Him. Release those things that you have been holding on to. God will lift those heavy weights off your shoulders. Remember, God is your friend, your father, lawyer, provider, healer, and deliverer. He is standing by waiting for you to talk to Him. He's been talking to you but you haven't been listening, so now He's leaving it up to you. If you are unsure what to say or how, just begin by telling Him about your day. Speak to Him as if you were speaking to one of your friends, because He is one of your friends.

Prayer

Father God I want to take this time to thank You for giving us breathe. I thank You for choosing to create us and give us life. I thank You for loving us so much that You gave Your only Son for our sins so that we may live for You. I thank You for having such a creative mind and creating the heavens and the earth. We appreciate You God and love You.

Amen

Testimony

I always find myself just asking God how He is feeling. I sit back and just say hi to Him. I truly care how God feels. I can feel Gods pain, my heart aches every time I think about how we hurt Him and disappoint Him. Have you ever just talked to God about Him or are all your conversations about you?

Share your testimony

_____

_____

_____

_____

_____

_____

_____

_____

_____

CHAPTER 5
You are Woman

No matter what anyone says
I made you in my image
I made the whole world first
To prepare it for you
I love you so much
I would do anything for you
I would wipe your weeping eyes
And mend your broken heart

You are woman
You're beautiful
You're divine

I want to give you my joy
Peace of mind you need
Allow me to set you free
All your burdens are cast away
My love you'll find
Inside you'll see

You are woman
You're beautiful

You're divine

You are worthy
Worthy to be loved
Just wait and see
I will send the one that I made
Just for you

Cause you are woman
You're beautiful
You're divine

✝

You are Woman Commentary

In the beginning God created man. "And God said, let us make man in our image, after our likeness: and let them have dominion over the fish of the sea, and over the fowl of the air, and over the cattle, and over all the earth, and over every creeping thing that creepeth upon the earth." (Genesis 1:26 KJV) Women we are so special that God created the heavens and the earth, all living creatures, plants, food, and even man before he brought us on the scene. He did not want man to be alone so he decided to bring us forth. But unlike the way he created Adam he decided to create us a little different. He took a rib from Adam and then shaped and molded us until we stood before him. "The man gave names to all the cattle, and to the birds of the sky, and to every beast of the field, but for Adam there was not found a helper suitable for him. So the Lord God caused a deep sleep to fall upon the man, and he slept; then He took one of his ribs and closed up the flesh at that place. The Lord God fashioned into a woman the rib which He had taken from the man, and brought her to the man. The man said, 'This is now bone of my bones, and flesh of my flesh; She shall be called woman, Because she was taken out of Man. 'For this reason a man shall leave his father and his mother, and be joined to his wife; and they shall become one flesh. And the man and his wife were both naked and were not ashamed." (Genesis 2:20-25 NASB Quick Study Bible) We are each unique and one of kind. We are all beautiful in our own special way.

There are women who have the perfect skin, so soft, and pure. Some women have beautiful flowing hair. Some have eyes that can melt any heart. Some have the most beautiful smile it can light up a room. Some have the most beautiful voice that the angels in heaven rejoice. We each have something that is beautiful about us. Too many women concentrate on their flaws or someone else's flaws instead of concentrating on their beauty. We need to begin to build one another up instead of tearing each other down. We have women fighting over men that don't even want them. We have women fighting over nonsense and teaching it to their daughters. We have women who have forgotten their worth. Do you know who you are? Women are strong. Women are sisters, daughters, aunts, wives, mothers, employees, and ministry workers. Women are the pillar of every great nation. There are so many strong women in the bible that stood out amongst the rest: Rebekah, Sara, Ruth, Mary, Mary Magdalene, Naomi, and Esther. There were other women that were mentioned, but these stood out the most because of their great deeds, sacrifices, strength and dedication to God and their faith.

Ladies do you want to be remembered by how many lap dances you gave? Or how many men you slept with? Or you might want to be remembered by the fights you were in? Oh yeah maybe it's important to know how many designer clothes and purses you own. How about how big your house is or how nice your car is. Maybe it's important to know that you worked out in the gym every day to maintain that beautiful figure you have so you can show it off with the tightest, shortest dress. God remembers us from the time he took that rib and shaped us into this beautiful woman that is full of potential. He remembers how he placed each talent and gift in us to become a born leader as a woman, mother, wife, minister of the word, and servant. We are more than what we think we are. We are not made to be a doormat, a punching bag, or some lost puppy. We were made to rise up and step out. God wants to bless each one of us with a husband, children, wealth, happiness, and everlasting life. We can have all and more by realizing who we are in God and what our purpose is.

Do you know what your purpose is? Do you know who you are? All women of different races, sizes, education backgrounds, financial status, housing status, past, and whatever else that makes us women; are beautiful, amazing, majestic, and divine. Stand daughters of the Most High God, lift your heads up, stand tall, and know who your Father is! God loves you and wants to give you His best. Are you ready to receive His best? Are you ready to lay down those things of the world to gain those things from heaven?

"She girds herself with strength and makes her arms strong. She senses that her grain is good; her lamp does not go out at night. She stretches out her hands to the distaff and her hands grasp the spindle. She extends her hand to the poor, and she stretches out her hands to the needy." (Proverbs 31:17-20 NASB Quick Study Bible) Ladies do you see who we are and who God wants us to be? Love each other today and stop the violence. Don't allow the enemy to continue to divide us and tear us apart. Open your eyes ladies and see what the enemy is doing to us. Be kind today, love a lady today, open your heart today and show a woman or a young girl some love. Tell them you love them and don't just say it, but mean it. I love you ladies with my whole heart.

Prayer

Father God I pray for your daughters today. I pray that each one of them begin to see their beauty the way you see it. I bind lust, abuse, and the attack on their minds. I erase every negative spoken or non-spoken word against them. I declare freedom from mental abuse, verbal abuse, physical abuse, and sexual abuse. I bind the desire to fight and be aggressive. Give them the desire to fight for you Lord. Daughters rise up and take your place as the princess of the King. Glory to God.

Amen

Testimony

I grew up a plus size girl and still remain a plus size woman. I have always had low self-esteem and hated the way I looked. I disliked my gap, my light skinned with scares, my weight and my lack of style when it came to dressing. I also grew up as a tom boy and I never learned how to properly dress for my body type and my style. I am still struggling in that area but I know I will get it together one day. God as truly opened my eyes about women and how important we are. I look at all of us in a different way now and realize that we are all beautiful in our own way. I may not have the perfect beach body, or perfect straight teeth, or the perfect skin, but I have found things I do like about me. I like my brown eyes, my height, my personality, my talent to write and create, and my ability to make others laugh. So I have grown to recognize that beauty is not just on the outside but also in the inside. I thank God for my beauty and how He has created me.

Share your testimony

_____

_____

_____

_____

_____

_____

_____

_____

_____

CHAPTER 6
To Be You

I can't imagine how it felt to be you
To face everything you went through
To be committed, to be true in everything that you do
You are awesome Lord
There is no one like you
I heard you whispering my name telling me
Just come and everything will be alright
Just come and don't give up the fight
Just come to me, just come, I AM.

You blessed me just for worshipping your name
You loved me even when I didn't love myself
You care for me when I wanted to give up everything
You said stay strong
Don't give up the fight
I heard you whispering my name telling me
Just come and everything will be alright
Just come and don't give up the fight
Just come to me, just come, I AM.

✝

To Be You Commentary

We are often faced with trials and tribulations throughout our life. But can you imagine how it felt to be whipped, cut, spit on and hung on a cross for someone else's sins? We are constantly asking why me Lord! God say's; "why not you"? He sent His only son here on this earth to be born of a virgin to walk in flesh to save this sinful world. But there were many who did not believe who He was and they decided to crucify Him. (John 19 KJV) So if Jesus can go through all of that for us why can't we go through?

God honors our worship, praise, faith and belief, but it's more appreciated when it's selfless. Have you just worshipped God for just who He is, not for what He can or what He has done for you? God deserves all of our praise and worship in the good and the bad. "Giving thanks always for all things unto God and the Father in the name of our Lord Jesus Christ;" (Ephesians 5:20 KJV).

We have moments when we feel like nothing is going right. Why does it seem as though everyone else is being blessed but me? Why does it seem like I'm always going through? It seems as though we have more downs then ups. Depression may set in. We feel stressed and overwhelmed.

But God is here to take all these burdens and make our days brighter. "Come unto me, all ye that labour and are heavy laden, and I will give you rest. Take my yoke upon you, and learn of me; for I am week and lowly in heart: and ye shall find rest unto your souls. For my yoke is easy, and my burden is light." (Matthew 11:28-30 KJV) Christ has come to save, deliver, heal and set us free from the wiles of the devil. He already took everything to the cross with Him, all we have to do is have faith and believe that it's already done. "And Jesus said unto them, Because of your unbelief: for verily I say unto you, if ye have faith as a grain of mustard seed, ye shall say unto this mountain, Remove hence to yonder place; and it shall remove; and nothing shall be impossible unto you." (Matthew 17:20 KJV) God is waiting for us to step out on faith. God allows many situations and circumstances to happen to see how faithful we are. Will you stand on God's word no matter what or who you're faced with? Will you continue to stand when things get really hard and it seems like there is no way out? Will you continue to share the good news of Jesus Christ when faced with death? How much do you really love God? These are some questions we all need to ask ourselves when faced with adversities. Stand strong my brother's and sister's because the outcome is better than the struggle. The struggle won't last always.

We read the scriptures of how Jesus was tormented before they hung Him on the cross. While reading those stories did we truly understand and see what really happened? Even having visuals of movies like "The Passion of Christ" portrayed the hate and denial from the people towards Jesus. How do you feel when you read what He did for us? How did you feel after watching the movie (if you viewed it)? If it

49

came down to it could you continue to praise God and deny yourself even to the cross? Have you laid" self down" and picked up your cross? Are you ready to die to self and become more like Christ? God is waiting for you my brother and sister to join Him in everlasting life.

To be you Jesus and do what you did for us is an honor no one can top. You deserve more than just our praise and worship, you deserve all of us. Lord no one has ever done what you have done for us. No one will ever do what you have done. So why brothers and sisters do you worship other god's, people and things? Why are all these other things more important to you than our Lord?

Don't turn your back on God and he won't turn His back on you. Read the word of God and learn who God truly is. See the sacrifice that He made for us. See the love that He showed to the people and how He is anticipating his return to join us with Him in heaven. Open your heart to see how it was to be Jesus.

Prayer

Heavenly Father I ask you to build your people's faith and belief in you. I pray that they begin to see signs and wonders of your great power. I pray that healing and deliverance begin to take place in their lives. I pray that they begin to worship and praise you for just because of whom you are. I pray when they give you thanks that it is selfless and with a pure heart. I pray that they begin to recognize you in all they do. In Jesus mighty name.

Amen

Testimony

I received Christ as my Lord when I was eighteen. My spiritual foundation started and began to grow thru the years. I read the scriptures and saw many different movies when it came to God and the bible. I was told several stories about how Christ was crucified, but when I had the opportunity to go the "Passion of Christ" I have never been the same. The depiction that was shown in the movie is one that will never leave my mind, my heart or my spirit. I cried so much watching that movie, but I have not been able to watch it again. My heart has been broken ever since and I cry out in pain for what they did to Him. He didn't deserve that. I will always stand for Christ and live my life for Him. God I thank you for your love and for your sacrifice.

Share your testimony

_____

_____

_____

_____

_____

_____

_____

_____

_____

_____

CHAPTER 7
Hold On

Hold on to you Lord
I got to hold on
Hold on to you Lord

O my first mistake was
I tried to do it on
I tried to do it on my own
But now, I know that I can't
Do it without you
Without you I will fall down
So Lord, I'm down on my knees
Begging you please
To stay by my side
So I'll stay strong

Hold on to you Lord
I got to hold on
Hold on to you Lord

O, you carried me through
The deep dark storm
Into the marvelous light
Lord, I seek your face

Like never before
I reverence your name
Cause, you are the most High

Hold on to you Lord
I got to hold on
Hold on to you Lord

† Hold On Commentary

We are always trying to do things on our own and in our own way. Sometimes pride can prevent us from asking for help rather it's from another individual or from God. We need to break that pride and begin to ask for help. "Pride goeth before destruction, and a haughty spirit before a fall." (Proverbs 16:18 KJV) God just wants us to hold on and to not give up. "Hold your peace, let me alone, that I may speak, and let come on me what will." (Job 13:13 KJV) God carries us through every test and trial. He wants us to constantly seek His face and build a relationship with Him. In order to have a relationship with God we must remain in our word daily, pray daily, and talk to Him daily. We must not be afraid to tell God what is on our mind. God already knows what we are thinking and feeling before we even have a thought or a feeling. Remember He knows are beginning and ending. The enemy makes us feel guilty, ashamed, and condemned of our past and everything that God has freed us from. When God forgives us it is no longer remembered. "He will turn again, he will have compassion upon us; he will subdue our iniquities; and thou wilt cast all their sins into the depths of the sea." (Micah 7:19 KJV)

When we feel like we want to give up and give in God is right there to pick up all the pieces. God is our Father, mother, brother, sister, friend, lawyer, judge, or whatever we need Him to be. All we have to do is call on His name. "Let your conversation be without covetousness; and be content with such things as ye have: for he hath said, I will never leave thee, nor forsake thee." (Hebrews 13:5 KJV) We are the one who leaves and turn our backs on Him. That is when we backslide and turn back to our wicked ways. Repent my brothers and sisters and turn from your wicked ways and return to God. "But seek ye first the kingdom of God, and his righteousness; and all these things shall be added unto you." (Matthew 6:33 KJV)

Hold on to the Lord and don't let Him go. He has already won the battle for us when he defeated death and took the keys from Satan. Now we just need to walk in victory and walk up right before the Lord. God has left us the manual (the Bible) to walk a saved and upright life. Jesus left us the comforter (the Holy Ghost) to help keep us saved. Yes we may make many mistakes, but God will use it for His good. Yes we will have test and trials, but they come to make us strong.

Hold fast to the horns of the altar. Don't let go in any circumstance. The enemy will taunt you with many temptations. Our flesh may fall weak sometimes, but we must pick ourselves back up, ask for forgiveness and keep pressing. You may feel alone at times and like no one cares. You may feel like things aren't getting any better. You may feel like you are in a deep hole and you just can't climb out. But I am here to tell you that there is a way out. Satan wants us to believe that we will never be happy, have a husband or wife, have a family, have a good job or career, loose the weight, have a nice house, have a nice car, or anything that we may desire. He wants to keep us low, because he knows how strong we will become when we hold on to God and hold on to the word of God and stand on it. Satan has already been defeated by Christ. He has no power. The power that he does have is what we give him. He can't do anything to us without our permission. We invite him into our lives when we sin. Hold on to the Lord, to his love and to your faith and tell the enemy he has no place in your heart, soul, or mind.

Also hold on to those around you that is positive, god fearing saint's. We are always trying to hold on to people because we are scared to let them go; we love them, and will feel bad if we let them go. This is the time that we don't have to hold on. Stop holding on to negative people, people that continue to live a worldly life style, individuals who mock your beliefs and God, and individuals who don't truly care about you. Stop keeping people in your life that hurt you and mean you no good. Be free today from all things that are holding you down and keeping you stuck in a paralyzed state of mind.

Prayer

Father God I pray for your people today that they will continue to hold on no matter how hard it may seem. God give your people the strength to endure and stand strong. Lord, help your people to open their spiritual eyes and begin to see themselves as you see them. I pray that your people begin to seek your face above all things and in all things they do. God I thank you for your love, your grace and your mercy. I thank you for guiding your people down the path

59

of righteousness and renewing a right spirit within them. In Jesus mighty name.

Amen

Testimony

I have been through many disappointments, heart aches, and pains, but even through all of that I have held on. There were several times I wanted to give up and just end it all. Due to sexual abuse as a child I tried to commit suicide a few times, but something prevented me from taking my own life. Then when I was 28 I attempted to take my life again. I had gotten into trouble with the law. I had never committed any crime or had any dealings with the law (except for a speeding ticket) and this was a very scary moment for me. I was angry at myself, embarrassed, I was full of shame and guilt, and didn't want to face the world. I was sitting in my house with a pile of pills laying on my table, door locked, all curtains and blinds closed, and ready to take my life. I was crying and felt so alone. But right at that moment there was a knock at my door and I heard the voice of God say, "It is not time for you to leave this world, I have more for you to do. You have a purpose and I have a plan for your life." I proceeded to open my door and my Pastor (Apostle Arnell Smith) stood there with open arms to check on me to ensure I was okay. My life was spared that day and I was given another chance to make a difference in my life and to help others who have fallen into similar situations such as I. Ever since that moment I have held on and not given up. Even in the midst of hard times, test and trials I continue to stand and press towards the mark of the high calling of Christ Jesus.

Share your testimony

_____

_____

_____

_____

_____

_____

_____

_____

_____

_____

CHAPTER 8

I Keep Running

I keep running, running, running
Away from you
Trying to hide, hide, hide
Not knowing what else to do
You gave me mercy, mercy, mercy
For my sick sinful soul
You showed me love, love, love
When I couldn't give no more

You gave me love, peace, joy and happiness
They all come from you
You gave me boldness and endurance
To fight life's temptations too
You are awesome in everything
For you are God, mighty, mighty, mighty
Awesome you are

But I keep running, running running
Away from you
Trying to hide, hide, hide
Not knowing what else to do
You gave me mercy, mercy mercy
For my sick sinful soul

You showed me love, love, love
When I couldn't give no more

✝

I Keep Running Commentary

When life feels like it's on our shoulders we drink our sorrows away. When alcohol can't sooth the problems anymore we turn to drugs. We start off with marijuana just to calm us, then when that doesn't calm anymore we begin to introduce stronger drugs to try and paralyze us from life itself. Each day we are losing ourselves to drugs and alcohol. But for those that doesn't know or understand we run to other things that may make us feel better for that time being. Many of us run to food, sex, pornography, over working, shopping (spending money) just to name a few.

We have those that run from church because of different reasons as well. There have been individuals who have been church hurt. Members of the congregation or possibly the leaders have verbally hurt them. Gossiping is the biggest killer. Maybe they pushed the individual out by not loving them. Church is a place of refuge, healing, deliverance, help, love, forgiveness, and understanding not a place that condemns you and make you feel worse than what you did in the world. "You shall not hate your fellow countryman in your heart; you may surely reprove your neighbor, but shall not incur sin because of him. You shall not take vengeance, nor bear any grudge against the sons of your people, but you shall love your neighbor as yourself; I am the Lord." (Leviticus 19:17-18 KJV) Your neighbor is not just the people who live next door to you or in your neighborhood, but anyone who you come across. We are to love everyone the way Christ loves us.

When someone hasn't been to church in a while do we bother to check on them and let them know we are thinking about them and how important they are to the body? Does anyone pray and try to find out why they haven't been there? How far are we willing to go to ensure our neighbor is okay and if there is anything we can do to get them back to God? Majority of the time people backslide because of what someone said to them, or what was not said. As believers of Jesus Christ we must have wisdom on how we should deal with others. We might think we are doing the right thing but sometimes we can say too much or not enough. Pray before you speak. Most importantly don't bring your personal issues or vendetta's into someone else's situations.

It's time to stop running from God. It's time to run to Him. Our past is our testimony. We have all fallen short and sinned. We are not perfect. We all make mistakes, some more than others. No one is holier than thou, even though they want you to think so. Even those that spit scripture like there is no tomorrow, aren't perfect. Knowing the bible from cover to cover don't make you saved, going to church every Sunday don't make you saved, wearing dresses everyday don't make you saved and singing in the choir don't make you saved. Confessing your sin's, proclaiming that Jesus Christ is Lord and he died on the cross and rose in three days, asking for forgiveness, and believing that Christ is yet alive is what makes you saved. Now to stay saved is to be baptized in the Holy Ghost, turn from the temptations of the world, be renewed in your mind and stand on faith that you are saved, building a relationship with God and remaining in the word and becoming a doer of the word not just a seer.

The church is the hospital for the sick to come and get healed. Have you noticed that there are many who are still sick in your congregations because they don't either want to be free from their sin's, or you have not allowed them to feel comfortable enough to run to God. If they see division, clicking, or negativity in the midst they begin to question if they are in the right place. Also if you are not operating in the gifts how can they be free from those things that have them bound? So many souls want to run in to get what you got. But we hold them back from God because of our haphazard lives. God said get his house in order, his souls is crying out and need a place to run to. God said if you don't want to get it together then get out of the way.

This is not the time to run from God. Time is nearing for Christ to return and we must be ready to enter the gates of heaven. Brothers and sisters know that you are important, special, unique and one of a kind. There is a call and purpose on your life. God is speaking to you right now and He wants you to know that He hears you and sees you and is assuring you that He is here. Don't give up or give in, it's not over until God says it's over. Rise brother and sister and run into your destiny.

Prayer

Father God I pray for my brothers and sisters today that they will rise up. I pray that they will stop running from you but to you. I ask you to give them strength and the power to stand when adversities try to enter in. I bind the enemy from any evil deeds he is trying to plot and plan. I ask you to cover them with the blood. I bind suicide and murder. I pray for love, peace and joy. Send individuals to them that will shower them with your love and provide them with words of wisdom and understanding. God I thank you for answered prayer and touching your people even as they read this prayer.

Amen

Testimony

For many years I ran from my calling and from God. I first gave my life to God when I was eighteen years old. When I initially got saved I was there to please my big sister and to follow up behind her. My feelings got hurt every time I felt as though I displeased her or I didn't do something right. I back slid often because my flesh wasn't ready to settle down in the Lord and I wasn't serving the Lord for myself but for other people. But in March of 2014 I made up in my mind that I was ready to live for God for me. I returned to church, repented and gave my life back to God. I have been holding on to my salvation and pressing forward in my ministry. Because of my faith, belief, commitment, sacrifice, and drive God has been truly blessing me to help others reach their goals. I thank God that I haven't let go and I am yet holding on.

Share your testimony

_____

_____

_____

_____

_____

_____

_____

_____

_____

_____

No never
No never
Forget me
Forget me!

You showered your love Lord
And I am forever yours
Forever yours!

I long to see your face
To feel your warm embrace
To hear the tenderness of your voice
Calling out your name
To see the beauty of your home
Now I call my own
The streets of gold, riches untold
Mine now and forever more
Forever more.

No never
No never
Forget me
Forget me!

You showered your love Lord
and I am forever yours
Forever yours!
I long to praise your name
To lift you up
Higher than high
Given the highest praise
Singing, Hallelujah, Hallelu, Hallelujah!
Singing, Hallelujah, Hallelu, Hallelujah!

No never
No never
Forget me
Forget me!

You showered your love Lord
And I am forever yours
Forever yours!

You forgave all my sins
Now I am reborn again
I followed the steps you gave
Down the path you paved
I know it's hard
Don't give up
Cause eternity, is forever more
Forever more.

Singing, Hallelujah, Hallelu, Hallelujah!
Singing, Hallelujah, Hallelu, Hallelujah!

No never
No never
Forget me
Forget me!

You showered your love Lord
And I am forever yours
Forever yours!

† No Never Commentary

God even in all our sins you have never forgotten us.
"Let your conversation be without covetousness;
and be content with such things as ye have: for he hath said,
I will never leave thee, nor forsake thee." (Hebrews 13:5 KJV)
We are sinners by nature because we are fleshly beings. But
after we give our lives over to God and are baptized in the
Holy Ghost we have the power to stay saved and free of
sin. Daily we must renew our minds by getting in our word
daily and praying before the Lord. "The Lord shall send
upon thee cursing, vexation, and rebuke, in all that thou
settest thine hand unto for to do, until thou be destroyed,
and until thou perish quickly; because of the wickedness of
thy doings, whereby thou hast forsaken me." (Deuteronomy
28:20 KJV) God is there for us day and night. God never
sleeps or slumbers. Can you imagine never sleeping? God is
omnipresent (everywhere at the same time) and can see us
all and everything that is happening all at once. God doesn't
miss anything. How amazing is that? There is nothing that
we do that God doesn't know. You may think you're doing
something in secret but God knows what you're doing even
before you do it. He will also share that secret with someone
who is filled with the Holy Ghost to come to you for you to

repent and get your spirit right. God also says: "If ye forsake the Lord, and serve strange gods, then he will turn and do you hurt, and consume you, after that he hath done you good." (Joshua 24:20 KJV) God will not continue to be made fun of. He supplies us with his grace and mercy. He showers us with his love (agape love) that is like no other love.

So the question stand's, how many times have we turned our backs on God and left Him? What was your excuse for leaving God? How many times have you forgotten God? When you are blessed with deliverance, healing, miracles, and material blessings do you acknowledge who blessed you or do you take the credit? How often is God forgotten for our accomplishments? Do you honestly think you're the reason you have that job, bills are paid, food on your table or any other blessing that flows in your life? God doesn't need our praise or worship, we do. When we praise and worship God for all He has done for us it pleases him that we recognize where our blessings come from. This causes God to want to bless us more. Who wouldn't want to praise a loving God?

God has prepared a path for us to follow. Of course our flesh will go fighting, kicking and screaming, but our spirits is ready and willing to follow the things and ways of the Lord. "Watch and pray, that ye enter not into temptation: the spirit indeed is willing, but the flesh is weak." (Matthew 26:41 KJV) Our flesh desires the things of the world (the things that cause us to sin) and our spirit desires those things of God (that brings us closer to God). Sin is what separates us from the Lord. God desires a separated people that may live in the world but is not a part of it. That means, we are not to partake in worldly activities (drinking, partying, fornication, adultery, lying, etc.), we are not to intertwine in gossip and those things that hurt others. We are to love with God's love and treat everyone with kindness. "Ye have heard that it hath been said, Thou shalt love thy neighbor, and hate thine enemy. But I say unto you, love your enemies, bless them that curse you, do good to them that hate you, and pray for them which despitefully use you, and persecute you; That ye may be the children of your Father which is in heaven: for he maketh his sun to rise on the evil and on the good, and sendeth rain on the just and on the unjust." (Matthew 5:43-48 KJV) We pray and ask God to never forget us and keep us lifted but how many people have we forgotten and turned our backs on?

We are always calling out and asking God to bless us, to forgive us, to deliver us, to heal us, or do something for us, but how many others do we pray these same prayers for? Are our prayers always selfish and always about ourselves? God honors selfless prayers. Let's keep our brothers and sisters lifted at all times. Pray for strangers and even those that hate and persecute you. We need to stand in one accord and pray in unity for all. Be happy and full of joy when your fellow brother/sister is blessed because your selfless act will gain you a golden brick on the street to heaven. Stay strong and stay focused on the task at hand; saving souls, doing Gods work and living your life for God, and he will never forget thee.

Prayer

Father God I pray for your people today that they shall become selfless. I pray that they begin to walk according to your word and your way. That the desires of the world will fade away and the desires of the Lord will resonate in them. I pray that you show your face to them God and assure them that you are still there and you have not forgotten them. I pray that they hear your voice for a stranger they will not follow. I pray that they begin to show love to everyone as you will them to do and begin to bless others from the blessings you have bestowed upon them. Give them a heart to give and not expect. God I thank you for your people and the work you are doing in their lives at this very moment. In Jesus mighty name.

Amen

Testimony

Even in the midst of all my mess and junk God has never left me or forgotten me. I have turned my back on him and left him several times, but he still remained with me and kept me safe from all harm. I became spiritually aware of how God was working in my life when I back slid and I would see members of the church and I realized God was calling me back to serve him. My time was up from living an ungodly life. It was time for me to stop running. Each time I ran from God and went back to the world the same thing would happen when it was time for me to return: God would send a saint from the church. This time was different when I went back. This time I made up in my mind, heart and spirit that I was ready to live for God whole heartedly. I was still called by God, but I didn't need to see the saints of God to know I was

77

being called this time. You see you can't come to God unless he calls you. I thank God for being called. Now I have come in the knowledge that He has also chosen me to do a work for Him. I am humbled and honored to be a servant.

Share your testimony

_____

_____

_____

_____

_____

_____

_____

_____

_____

_____

CHAPTER 10
Inspired Love

Oh Love, you are so sweet.
Like the fluffy clouds in the sky.
Like each tear drop that falls from your eyes.
From the tenderness of your touch.
You make every day worth while.

Oh Love, you are the reason I rise.
Like the morning sun and like the evening moon.
Like the twinkling of each star.
From the delicateness of your voice.
You make every smile bright.

Oh Love, you are so pure.
Like the white sands at the beach.
Like the calmness of your spirit.
From each step you make.
You make the dark shine.

Oh Love, how you loved me first.
Like the intricate details of my creation.
Like the blessings you bestow.
From the way you never leave my side.

You Inspire me God forever more.

✝

Inspired Love Commentary

From the time a mother conceives her love for that baby begins. From every growing pain, sickness, stretch mark, and craving that mother loves that baby. Then that day comes when it is time for the baby to arrive and for the first time the mother sees his or her face and holds him/her in her arms, it is a bond that can't ever be broken. This is exactly what happened when God created us. He formed us from the dust and breathed life into us. How special is that. Have you ever wondered what inspired Him to create the heavens and the earth? What inspired Him to create the waters and the land? Where did He get the idea to create all the things that creep, crawl and live upon the earth and the waters? Then He had the idea to create man. Have you ever sat back and thought about how our bodies function and everything that makes us who we are? That is Love.

That kind of love inspires me to be better and do better. "And the King shall answer and say unto them, Verily I say unto you, inasmuch as ye have done it unto one of the least of these my brethren, ye have done it unto me." (Matthew 25:40 KJV) When we show love to the homeless, to the lost, to the broken and anyone that others pass by we are showing the love of Christ. Love may come natural for many but not for all, because all have not been shown love. There are some that have a difficult time to even receive love because they don't know if you are genuine or not. How lonely is that loveless journey? There are individuals who are not as affectionate as others either. You have those who love to hug and are very touchy feely. Then you have those who don't like to touch or hug, but are willing to shake your hand (lightly). You can't force people to be affectionate, either they are or they aren't. Yes I agree that those who are overly affectionate need to try and tone it down and those who aren't affectionate at all need to add a little into their diet.

God loves us so much that He assures that we have everything we could possibly need. "Therefore I say unto you, take no thought for your life, what ye shall eat, or what ye shall drink; nor yet for your body, what ye shall put on. Is not the life more than meat, and the body than raiment? Behold the fowls of the air: for they sow not, neither do they reap, nor gather into barns; yet your heavenly Father feedeth them. Are ye not much better than they? Which of you by taking thought can add one cubit unto his stature?" (Matthew 6:25-34 KJV) So you see God's love runs deeper then you can imagine. Does Gods love inspire you? Does it inspire you enough to love others the way He loves you? What does inspire you?

God loves us so much that even after we sinned He had Noah build an ark to save his family and two of every animal to make a fresh beginning. He brought forth a flood and destroyed everything and everyone that sinned and was disobedient to his commandments. Then after all that, sin found its way back to our people. God then decided He was going to make a final sacrifice to save his people by sending His Son through the Virgin Mary. Jesus came in the flesh to give hope to the lost, to heal, to deliver, to teach, and share the good news of God. He came to give Gods creation another chance to get saved and to turn from their wicked ways. But there were those who did not believe who He was and plotted to kill Him (crucify). The crucifixion was the final sacrifice and act of love shown by God. Jesus now waits for His second coming to gather Gods children to take them back to heaven. "For God so loved the world, that he gave his only begotten Son, that whosoever believeth in him should not perish, but have everlasting life." (John 3:16 KJV) "In this was manifested the love of God toward us, because that God sent his only begotten Son into the world, that we might live through him." (I John 4:9 KJV) Do you not see how much God loves us? Would you be able to sacrifice your child like that? What are you willing to do to have a personal, intimate relationship with God? What are you willing to lay down and let go? "And when he had called the people unto him with his disciples also, he said unto them, whosoever will come after me, let him deny himself, and take up his cross, and follow me." (Mark 8:34 KJV) God is waiting for us to deny self and live according to the word (Bible). The bible is a guide (manual) to live by and keep us saved. Jesus also left the comforter (the Holy Ghost) to remind us of the things of God, and to keep us holy, and to keep us in line with the word. It is up to us to live according to His word because He will never force Himself on us. How much do you truly love God? How far are you willing to go for God?

Prayer

Father God I pray that your people are filled with so much love that it just seeps thru their pores. I pray that they begin to show everyone they come in contact with the love of Christ. I pray that they are showed love like never before. I pray for those who have a hard time showing affection that they will begin to feel comfortable. I pray that each one of your people begin to appreciate everything around them that you have created. Begin to realize how much love and care you put into Your creation. God I thank You for loving us so much that You give us an opportunity each day we rise to get it right. God you inspire me and I pray you begin to inspire others. In Jesus mighty name. Amen

Testimony

Growing up I took a lot of things for granted. I hated everything and everyone. I was not happy and just wanted to end my life. I felt as though I didn't matter and no one would miss me or care if I was gone. But then I met a man. His name is Jesus and he came into my life and saved me. Jesus has taught me and showed me that I am beautiful, I am loved, and I have purpose. I now see life and everything around me with different eyes. I pay more attention to how the sky just stays up in the air and how the waters stay in their position. I admire how the trees grow and bring forth leaves and give us oxygen. I sit back and think about how God created us and how the intricate details of our being is so advanced. My love for God grows every day that he allows me to rise. I love Him more every time I gaze into my daughter's eyes. My love has also grown to appreciation. God is so amazing to me I can't help but to love and appreciate Him.

Share your testimony

_____

_____

_____

_____

_____

_____

_____

_____

_____

_____

CHAPTER 11
Set Apart for a Purpose

I have come to realize that I have purpose.
I have a great call on my life.
My trials and tribulations are not in vain.
God has removed individuals from my life.
I am to be alone with Him.
To build my relationship with Him.
To build my Spirit up in strength.
This is the season for growth, prosperity,
Maturity, longevity, endurance, and longsuffering.

I wanted friends to share my salvation with.
But God said no not yet.
He wants me in a place to send the right friends.
I am moving to higher ground and
Only those who are lifted up can and will
Stand with me in such a time as this.

I am prepared and ready to walk in the will of God.
I am ready to receive the blessings He as stored up for me.
I am ready to walk in victory.
Even if this means I am alone with only Him.

God is all I need, He is my everything.
I love you Lord for setting me apart for such a time as
this.

✝

Set Apart for a Purpose Commentary

To be set apart means that God has his hand on us for a specific purpose. Rather we like it or not God will begin to remove individuals and things out of our lives to set us apart. Your purpose may be greater than some and you will suffer and sacrifice more than they. But even those whose purpose isn't has great will have to suffer and sacrifice. "And we know that all things work together for good to them that love God, to them who are the called according to his purpose." (Romans 8:28 KJV) "To everything there is a season, and a time to every purpose under the heaven." (Ecclesiates 3:1 KJV) So has you can see there is a place and a time when our purpose will shine. If you don't know what your purpose is then begin to pray and seek God for your purpose. Another way to seek your purpose is to look at your passion. Does your passion please God? Your passion may be to dance. So instead of dancing for the world now you praise or mime dance and praise the Lord. You may love to sing. You now sing in the choir or a soloist for God instead of singing worldly music. You may enjoy writing, teaching, fixing cars, helping others, and so and so forth. Normally our passion lines up with our purpose.

When being set apart it can become a lonely journey. You will have individuals placed in your life for a season for a reason. After that season is over then you won't spend as much time with them as you used too. We are praying and asking God for a friend that we can pray with, study with and hang out sometimes, but God says: "No not yet, this is your time to be with Me." So you accumulate associates that you gather necessary information from for your purpose then when you have completed that task then they too shall be released from your life and it will be someone else's turn. The many relationships we encounter are a learning experience. This is our time to grow, mature and attain what we need to move forward in our purpose. Losing certain people is not easy but in order for us to move forward God will remove all distractions that are keeping us from doing what He has called us to do. God will fill our void of loneliness. When we become content where we are then God can finally bless us with our desires. Are you satisfied where you are?

"Thou shalt surely give him, and thine heart shall not be grieved when thou givest unto him: because that for this thing the Lord thy God shall bless thee in all thy works, and in all that thou puttest thine hand unto. " (Deuteronomy 15:10 KJV) Our works will also determine our purpose. God honors our works. In order to walk in your purpose there must be some action on your part. Are we all talk and no action? "But wilt thou know, O vain man, that faith without works is dead?" (James 2:20 KJV) It takes faith to step out into new territory. We must remember that we are not alone. Though Moses used the excuse of not speaking eloquently his purpose was to speak to Pharoh to free Gods people. God assured him that He would be with him just have faith and go. Noah was told to build an Ark and when the flood was over it was his purpose to repopulate the earth along with his family. You see we all have a purpose and God will be with

us the whole step through. He said He will never leave us. "Now faith is the substance of things hoped for, the evidence of things not seen." (Hebrews 11:1 KJV) We must continue to walk by faith and not by sight. (I Corinthians 5:7 KJV)

Since you have realized what your purpose is have you been able to rest? Has the enemy been attacking you more? Have you gained more enemies and lost more friends? Well you are headed in the right direction. We must lose in order to gain. If it is going too perfect, running real smooth, and nothing bad seems to be happening then you're works is not focused towards kingdom work. The enemy only attacks those who have laid their life down for the Lord. "And the Lord said unto Satan, hast thou considered my servant Job, that there is none like him in the earth, a perfect and an upright man, one that feareth God, and escheweth evil? And still he holdeth fast his integrity, although thou movedst me against him, to destroy him without cause." (Job 2:3 KJV) Let's find our purpose today and begin to walk into our destiny.

Prayer

Father God I thank You for Your people and finding them worthy to set them apart from the rest. God I pray that they find their purpose and walk into their destiny. Please give them the strength to face all test and trials. Give them the grace to endure all sufferings and sacrifices that they will face during the process. Give them peace God in their minds and hearts has they dive into the unknown. I bind the enemy from any attacks he may try to encounter. He has no place here. God I thank You for what You are doing for Your people.

Amen

Testimony

I have asked several times for God to send me a saved friend that I can pray with, hang out with and chat with some times. I have been blessed to have several people come into my life. Each one of these people had come into my life for a purpose and for a season. We have been an asset for one another and provided valuable spiritual guidance that the other may have needed. God told me very clearly that this is not my season to have friends around me. I am to be alone with Him and build my relationship with Him and only Him. There are many times I feel alone. I know God is there, but I desire to have a physical person around I can talk to sometimes. God has set me apart because of the calling on my life. The position He is placing me in will cause me to be alone a lot and would cause conflict with trying to have a friend at this present time. I have to learn to be friends with God and walk into my destiny. I am grateful that God chose me to be set apart for such a time as this.

Share your testimony

_____

_____

_____

_____

_____

_____

_____

_____

_____

_____

CHAPTER 12

I'm Still Standing

I have been molested and emotionally abused.
I used alcohol, marijuana, and sex
As a way of escape.
I allowed men to use me
And didn't take pride in who I was.
I've been abused and used.
I've been lied to and lied on.
I've been cheated on and mistreated.
I've been talked about and backslidden.
I've been stressed and depressed.
I've been broke and broken.
I've been tried and convicted.
But I'm STILL STANDING.
With God I'm still holding on.
With every breath I take.
With every thought I think.
With every step I make.
I AM STILL STANDING.

✝

I'm Still Standing Commentary

We have all walked down different paths. We continue to walk down our own separate paths and it is set on a journey to get to our destiny. Some have suffered more than others because of the call on their life, but it does not mean their suffering is more important than another. There have been individuals who remain in bondage from molestation. You no longer have to walk with this embarrassing, lonely, shameful demon. You can be free today and walk in victory. The first step is to forgive the person who has crossed the line and took your innocence from you. I know you may ask, "Why am I forgiving them after what they did to me?" Well the forgiveness isn't just for them but it is for you. "So shall ye say unto Joseph, forgive, I pray thee now, the trespass of thy brethren, and their sin; for they did unto thee evil: and now, we pray thee, forgive the trespass of the servants of the God of thy father. And Joseph wept when they spake unto him." (Genesis 50:17 KJV) We can't enter into the gates of heaven with unforgiveness in our hearts. God has forgiven us of all our sins, so why can't we forgive those who have trespassed against us? We are to love everyone, including our enemies.

Have you had issues with alcohol, cigarettes and drugs?

You can be free from those habits as well. These are distractions from the enemy to keep you bound and out of the will of God. If you are under the influence you can't understand the things of God. You don't need these things to make you happy or to have a good time. There is joy, love, happiness and peace in Jesus. You can have a Holy Ghost party and it is the best feeling you will ever experience. "Know ye not that the unrighteous shall not inherit the kingdom of God? Be not deceived: neither fornicators, nor idolaters, nor adulterers, nor effeminate, nor abusers of themselves with mankind, nor thieves, nor convetous, nor drunkards, nor revilers, nor extortioners, shall inherit the kingdom of God." (I Corinthians 6: 9-10 KJV) We are to be sober so we can hear from God and be able to do His will.

Are you having issues with fornicating, homosexuality or masturbation? You can be free from that lust demon as well. We were created to be with one man and one woman in marriage. Our purpose is to reproduce and populate the earth. We can't reproduce if we are masturbating or having intercourse with the same sex. "Now concerning the things whereof ye wrote unto me: it is good for a man not to touch a woman. Nevertheless, to avoid fornication, let every man have his own wife, and let every woman have her own husband. Let the husband render unto the wife due benevolence: and likewise also the wife unto the husband." (I Corinthians 7 KJV) It doesn't talk about having more than one husband or wife, or having same sex marriage. Sex is between husband and wife. The enemy has deceived us with pornography, movies, and other images of lust that make it seem enticing and good. Be free from that demon today and walk according to the word of God.

People are going to continue to lie to us, hurt us, use us,

and be mean to us as long as we live here on this earth. The enemy doesn't rest because we get saved. When we make the decision to give our lives to God the enemy attacks us more because he wants us to turn back to his kingdom. Don't give up my brothers and sisters and allow the enemy victory over your life. God has your back and is always here for you. You don't have to be stressed or depressed today. Lay those things down at the altar. Allow God to fight your battles for you. Don't be afraid to say you can't handle it and ask God to take the reins. "Fight the good fight of faith, lay hold on eternal life, whereunto thou art also called, and hast professed a good profession before many witnesses." (I Timothy 6:12 KJV) "And Joshua said unto them, Fear not, nor be dismayed, be strong and of good courage: for thus shall the Lord do to all your enemies against who ye fight." (Joshua 10:25 KJV)

Test and trials come to build us up and make us stronger. Yes they can take a toll on our spirits and our bodies but we are still standing. After being molested, beaten, broken, hurt, used, abused, lied on, cheated on, and left behind we are still standing. Learn from each experience. Keep your head held high and know that there is better to come. God has not forgotten you. Your time is coming for a blessing. Allow God to heal and deliver you today of those things that keep you bound. Allow God to pour joy, peace and love into you. Be free today and walk in victory because through it all you are still standing.

Prayer

God your people have been bound and chained with sins, hurts, and unforgiveness for many years. I pray that they are released today. I bind depression, stress, unforgiveness, lust, overeating, lying, laziness, selfishness, and all sins that are keeping my brother and sister from having a full life with You Lord. I pray that the burdens of the world are lifted up off their shoulders and that they may walk in victory. I pray that their eyes will be opened to the deceptions of the enemy and they will not fall into his traps. I pray that they desire the things of You God and turn from their wicked ways. God I thank You for freeing your people today, in Jesus mighty name.

Amen

Testimony

I have suffered molestation, unforgiveness, masturbation, verbal abuse, mental abuse, alcohol, marijuana, lust, fornication, lying, being cheated on, misused, left, and heart broken. But with God's help I am still standing. It was not an easy journey and it took some time to be free from most of these sins, but once I was aware that I was still carrying these loads I was able to get free from them. I walk in victory today from these demons that kept me bound. I am not perfect, I still sin, but I have the tools now to know how to ask for forgiveness and stay free. I don't give any power to the enemy I stand in victory and walk with my head held high.

Share your testimony

_____

_____

_____

_____

_____

_____

_____

_____

_____

_____

CHAPTER 13
I Remain in Love

From day one when God decided to create me I was full of love. As I entered into this harsh cruel world I remained full of love. Even through heartache, lies, abuse and mistrust from those closets's to me I remain full of love. Hidden now deep in my heart waiting for the one to resurrect it from death. In search of the one I surrounded myself with pretenders of the one. Still focusing on the day I will be swept off my feet. I continue to envision that day of Holy matrimony but realizing it will never be my ending. After drawing images of my gown, taking snap shots of my guy, I still wait for the one. Search after search I remain in wait for the one. I gave my heart and soul to one, but through it all he was not the one. So I remain continuously on this journey of singleness for he that God has created especially for me. I then become involved with one that blessed me with a child. Once again I am excited, anticipating the day we will become one in marriage. With broken promises and several lies he too proved to be not the one. I still remain full of love and waiting for the one. I have a heart overflowing that wants to shower the one with more love than he has ever known. The love I share is that of Christ who went to the cross for love. The love I share is that of God who created the heavens and earth with a spoken word of love. I no longer want to be surrounded by pretenders, imitations, or false creations of the one. I want the one that God shaped and molded just for me and I for him. I am one of his bone and flesh of his flesh. When our hands interlock the electricity that transcends will light up the sky. I will not slip into temptation because my flesh is lonely. I will not fall for the traps of a ones lies. I will keep my spiritual eyes stayed on Jesus and walk hand in hand with the Lord that there will be no more maybe's but finally a defiantly. So I am waiting for the one so I can grant him with my touch of love that God has overflowed in me like a rushing waterfall. So I will continue to stand still and pray, prepare and remain until the one finds me full of God's love.

✝

I Remain in Love Commentary

Do you have a desire to be married and live happily ever after? Well I don't know about the happily ever after part, but marriage can be in the cards for you. Marriage is sacred and should not be entered into lightly and under false pretenses. Yes you may get lonely and want someone to share your life with. You may want someone you can pray with, pray for and him or her pray for you. You may want someone that you can work in ministry with or who will stand by your side as you walk in you ministry. Whatever your heart desires be sure that you are equally yoked and desire the same things for your lives. "Be ye not unequally yoked together with unbelievers: for what fellowship hath righteousness with unrighteousness? And what communion hath light with darkness?" (II Corinthians 6:14 KJV) If you are single just allow yourself to grow and mature in the Lord. Study Proverbs 31 and allow yourself to mature as the woman of God he created you to be. Men you can also study about the Proverbs 31 woman so you can see whom God desires for you to marry.

God created and designed us to love and be in love. God

is love (agape love) and He created us with love. God never wanted us to hurt, be heart broken or alone. The enemy steps in and we are faced with abuse and the mindset to want to be alone or to settle. Don't settle for just anyone so you aren't alone because that will just bring more misery. Wait on God to bless you with your Boaz or Ruth. God desires for you to be happy and blessed. Yes being alone can sometimes be lonely but it allows you to get to know who you are and to know who God is.

Even in the midst of you waiting for the one God has created especially for you ask God to keep you full of His love. Know that you are loved and that love will find you. It's okay to desire to be married and to be happy. It is okay to envision your dream wedding and a life time of happiness. It is okay to want more and to not want to be alone. God tells us to be honest with our feelings. He already knows how we feel anyway we just need to be honest with ourselves.

We have all been in relationships rather they were good or bad. Something didn't go right because otherwise we wouldn't be single. One of the biggest mistakes is that we blame the other person all the time instead of taking responsibility for our own actions. It takes two to have a relationship and if you have entered the relationship with the wrong intentions it's not going to work. One of the biggest downfalls of a relationship is that God is not the head of it. Even in our friend and family relationships we must learn to love with God's love. God will allow us to be in situations to test our love, patience, kindness and respect towards others. This is also preparation for marriage. When you unite in marriage you are welcoming all the positive and negatives of that other person in your life. We are not perfect, we are all flawed, so don't expect anyone to change after you have said

"I Do". Marriage won't change a person, only a person can decide to change if they choose too.

Have you been single for some time now? Have you been praying and asking God to bless you with a husband or wife? Know that he hears you and that your praying is not in vain. There is a reason that you have not been introduced to your Boaz or Ruth, for this is your season to prepare and study on how to be a wife/husband for the one. Don't settle for a one when the one is preparing for you. No it is not easy to wait, but God will honor you in your waiting. Continue to walk in unconditional love and before you know it the one will be greeting you with forever love. Don't waste your time entertaining imitations of the one and giving your heart and emotions to a one that will only break it and hurt you. Stand on God's word and faith that the one is seeking you as well and preparing for you. "Whoso findeth a wife findeth a good thing, and obtaineth favour of the Lord." (Proverbs 18:22 KJV) Ladies it is not your responsibility to seek your husband but to be ready when he arrives. Rather we know it or not there is a man watching us to see if we are wife material. Let's not give him any reason to pass us by.

God always keeps his promises. He can't lie. If God promised that you will be married then you will. But know this, if you are not married while here on this earth you will be married in heaven. All blessings will not take place here on this earth. Don't get discouraged and don't give up, continue to live upright and righteous before the Lord and your sacrifices will be rewarded. Be blessed in your waiting.

Prayer

Lord this is a prayer for all Your single women and men who are seeking a mate. There are many who have been single for quite some time and question why they are alone. They are living according to Your word and have walked with You for years. They see others getting married while they remain single. Doubt has begun to set in their hearts and this is when they begin to settle for whoever crosses their path. God I pray that You continue to give them the strength to stand on Your word and for them not to settle. They deserve to be treated like kings and queens. They deserve to be loved unconditionally. They deserve to have the desires of their hearts. I bind the enemy from bringing forth any distractions and false pretenses. I ask You Lord to lift up Your people and feel them with Your love Lord. Show them that they are special and important and deserves Your best. Continue to guide them down the road of righteousness and protect their hearts from being broken. Keep their emotions under control and allow them to be led by the Spirit and not their loneliness. God I thank You for keeping Your people and giving them direction. In Jesus mighty name I pray.

Amen

Testimony

I have been heartbroken many times. I grew up looking for love in all the wrong places and most of those places were through men who didn't want me. Or should I say they didn't want a relationship with me, they just wanted sex. When I was 17years of age I gave my heart to one who became my husband and he hurt me so deeply. He had very good qualities and had the potential to be a great husband, but he had some baggage that he couldn't let go. We both entered the marriage for the wrong reasons. I gave my life to the Lord and did not want to fornicate or shake up and he didn't want to lose me so we ended up married. Well that didn't end well. Then years after that I continued my search but only ended up empty handed. Then while in a backslidden state I met a man that blessed me with my beautiful little girl. I knew from the beginning we were unequally yoked. Even in my backslidden state I still had desires and expectations for my life and now my daughter's life. I wanted to be married and he did not. Under life changing situations he proposed to me. I accepted instead of walking away. Then as time went on he finally admitted he was not ready. Well I had to walk away, because I refuse to play house and wife and we aren't married. So here I am again picking up the pieces from my broken heart, raising my daughter alone and trying to be a good role model for her. But I have decided that I will wait for the one and not settle anymore for a one. I now know who I am and what I deserve. I will continue to stand on God's promises for my life and wait for my Boaz. I know there is a man out there for me that was created just for me. I will wait.

Share your testimony

_____

_____

_____

_____

_____

_____

_____

_____

_____

_____

References

Foundation, T. L. (2006). NASB Quick Study Bible. La
   Habra: Thomas Nelson, Inc.
Hengeveld, N. (1993). Bible Gateway. Retrieved August
   17, 2015, from www.biblegateway.com: http://www.
   biblegateway.com

Thank You!

If you have read this book to this point, that means you have finished. I pray that these words ministered to you and answered any questions you may have had. I pray someone was saved, delivered, healed and set free from the holds of the enemy. I want to thank you for purchasing the book and taking time out to read it. Writing this book taught me to never give up on my dreams. This is just the beginning there is more to come. We must begin to walk out on faith and not concentrate on the negativity around us. The word also says: now faith is the substance of things hoped for and the evidence of things not seen. Just because you may not see things happening when you want it to happen does not mean it's not. I love you all and pray blessings upon you a thousand fold. Keep walking by faith and not by sight and know who you are in God. Keep pressing towards the high calling of Christ Jesus and walk into your destiny.

Respectfully,

Yolanda N. Harris

Journal Your Thoughts

About the Author

Yolanda N. Harris is a native of Rockford, IL who has one beautiful daughter (Keranie). She has experienced many trials and tribulations throughout her lifetime. With the guidance of God and her leadership from her church home, **Deliverance Crusaders Center**, along with her Bachelor's degree in Management and Leadership, certificate in Human Services and courses in Communications Management, she has grown naturally and spiritually. She uses her experiences to minister in the prison ministry where she provides study tools and support for those who have been forgotten by society. She has also created a magazine that is geared towards those that have felony records: *UnCommon Grounds Magazine*. She also began serving the children of the residents of IDOC to provide support and gifts for them for the holidays. Yolanda's passion is to be a servant to God, to encourage and uplift, and to motivate others to achieve their goals. God uses Yolanda's experiences to lead others that share similar situations to the Kingdom. Yolanda's desire is to lead God's people into a life of possibilities.